Asteroid Alley Games Guide

Cosmic City™ VBS
ASTEROID ALLEY GAMES GUIDE
Published by David C. Cook
4050 Lee Vance View
Colorado Springs, CO 80918 U.S.A.

David C. Cook Distribution Canada
55 Woodslee Avenue, Paris, Ontario, Canada N3L 3E5

David C. Cook U.K., Kingsway Communications
Eastbourne, East Sussex BN23 6NT, England

David C. Cook and the graphic circle C logo
are registered trademarks of Cook Communications Ministries.

ISBN 978-1-4347-9960-9

Cover Design: BMB Design
Interior Design: Sandy Flewelling, TrueBlue Design
Art: Aline Heiser, Mark Stay, Russell Tate
Photographs: © Brad Armstrong Photography

All Scripture quotations, unless otherwise stated, are from THE HOLY BIBLE, NEW
INTERNATIONAL VERSION. Copyright © 1973, 1978, 1984 by International Bible Society.
Used by permission of Zondervan Publishing House. All rights reserved.

Thanks to our gifted development team!
Rebekah Atkinson, Jeff Barnes, Mary Grace Becker, Cheryl Crews, Leigh Davidson, Caroline Ferdinandsen, Diane
Gardner, Nancy Haskins, Jodi Hoch, Kate Holburn, Sharron Jackson, Janet Lee, Marcia Lioy, Douglas Mauss, Scot
McDonald, Susan Miller, Kevin Mullins, Carol Pitts, Jan Pendergrass, Karen Pickering, Loreta Riddle, Gail Rohlfing,
Christina Schofield, Sheila Seifert, Judi Tippie, Kelli Trujillo, and Dawn Renee Weary.

Printed in China

transforming lives, together

Welcome to Cosmic City!

No mission could be more exciting—or vital—than drawing your young Space Voyagers closer to the Lord. We're pleased you've chosen to join Cosmic City Tours on this journey. You're embarking on an out-of-this-world adventure that brings the wonder of God to life.

During David C. Cook's 2008 Vacation Bible School, your Space Voyagers will join Cosmic City Tours on a journey through Cosmic City, a floating space city unlike anywhere else. In every corner of Cosmic City, God's wonder will dazzle the Voyagers' hearts and minds. They'll experience this awesome wonder in a new way every day at the city's stellar attractions. Children will experience God's awesome power with hands-on Bible dramas at the Theater of the Galaxies, rocket beyond our atmosphere with games at Asteroid Alley, create memorable crafts at SuperNova SuperMart, touch and feel the wonder of God at the Wonder U. Laboratory, worship the Creator of the Universe at Deeper Space, and fuel up with tasty snacks at The Shooting Star Drive-in.

We've given you everything you need to make this incredible week easy to plan and manage. This guide provides helpful suggestions and materials to transform each tour stop into a delightful place filled with vivid colors and retro-future décor. Every activity children participate in is founded on biblical teaching, ensuring that this space adventure will change lives.

Each location kids visit in the rotation comes with its own guide. Just follow the simple instructions in this guide and you're ready to go! Plus, you'll find more choices than ever. Whether you're guiding children through games, snacks, Bible dramas, crafts, learning labs, or music and Bible memory, you'll find multiple options and suggestions to choose from each day. This gives you complete freedom to customize your tour stop to suit the unique needs of your children.

Best of all, every child has a special place in this futuristic city. Preschool children can participate in *Cosmic City™: Blast Off!*, and kids in fourth and fifth grades can enjoy a more extreme exploration of the city through *Cosmic City™: Outer Limits*. These options give your church an opportunity to reach children at their own level. It'll enhance and optimize each Space Voyager's experience. And you'll find it makes VBS more manageable too!

Everything you need to get started is waiting for you in the pages ahead. So get ready for a week that will change lives and prepare for liftoff to *Cosmic City™*—where kids, and their leaders, explore the awesome wonder of God ... and never return the same.

—The David C. Cook VBS Development Team

Table of Contents

Cosmic City™ Debriefing (VBS Week Overview)

	BIBLE STORY	KEY VERSE	LIVE IT!	THEATER OF THE GALAXIES Bible Drama	SUPERNOVA SUPERMART Crafts	
Day 1	God's Wondrous Creation (Gen. 1:1—2:4; Ps.136:1–9, 25–26)	Psalm 90:2 Before the mountains were born or you brought forth the earth and the world, from everlasting to everlasting you are God.	God is awesome! I can worship him.	The actors are missing and the creation drama is about to begin! Meet the delightful friends who will help tell this awesome and wonderful story.	*Nature Tiles* or *Starry Wind Sock*	
Day 2	Desert Wonder: God Provided Manna, Quail, and Water for the Israelites (Ex. 16:1–17, 31–36; 17:1–6)	Isaiah 58:11 The LORD will guide you always; he will satisfy your needs.	God is awesome! I can count on him.	Two Israelites with differing opinions tell of God's desert provision. An unlikely interruption highlights God's faithfulness.	*Animal Sunglass Case* or *Quail Pail*	
Day 3	Healing Wonder: Jesus Heals a Paralyzed Man (Luke 5:17–26)	Psalm 77:14 You are the God who performs miracles; you display your power among the peoples.	God is awesome! I can believe in him.	A paralyzed man's friend shares a greater miracle that happened the day his friend was healed (forgiveness).	*Praise Mat* or *Crazy Comets*	
Day 4	Water Wonder: Jesus Walks on Water (Matt. 14:22–33)	Mark 10:27 All things are possible with God.	God is awesome! I can trust in him.	Theatrical disaster is narrowly avoided when everyone pitches in to tell how Jesus walked on water and calmed a stormy sea.	*Stormy Place Mat* or *Boat Mouse Pad*	
Day 5	The Wonder of God Brought Down to Earth: Jesus' Resurrection (John 19:1–6, 16–18; 20:1–8)	Philippians 3:10 I want to know Christ and the power of his resurrection.	God is awesome! I can tell others about Jesus.	Celebration breaks out when the world's worst day, the day of Jesus' death, leads to the world's best day, the day Jesus rose again.	*Cosmic Container* or *Space Log*	

4 **COSMIC CITY™ VBS** Asteroid Alley Games Guide

ASTEROID ALLEY Games	THE SHOOTING STAR DRIVE-IN: Snacks	DEEPER SPACE Bible Memory and Music	WONDER U Learning Lab	COSMIC CLUE QUEST
Creation Stations Reinforce today's Bible story with visits to seven Creation Stations. **String Creations** Use string to create symbols of God's wondrous creation.	Pizza Planets or Meteor Munch	"From Everlasting to Everlasting" (Praise Music and Video) Star Light, Star Bright or Battle Star (Key Verse Memory Activities)	Creating Beauty Out of Nothing Colors emerge from the color black, teaching that God can create beauty out of nothingness.	Location: Deeper Space Clue: I will praise you
Manna Madness Collect the "manna" without getting tagged by the opposing team. **Birds and Bread Blastoff** Keep feathers on heads, shoulders, knees, or noses while collecting "manna."	Modern Manna or Planet Pops	"God Will Meet My Needs" (Praise Music and Video) Manna Mania or Satellite Circle (Key Verse Memory Activities)	Old Faithful and Our Forever Faithful God A geyser spurts in unexpected ways, teaching kids to count on God to provide.	Location: Asteroid Alley Clue: O Lord
Mat Mix-up Get safely back "home" with your mat. **Mega Mats** Work together to make it "home" with your mat.	Sun Burst or Pudding Pop Walk	"My God Does Miracles" (Praise Music and Video) Balloon Blastoff or Miracle Mats (Key Verse Memory Activities)	Gravity vs. Our Amazing Reflexes Kids learn that they can trust God, who holds the world in place and made their amazing bodies.	Location: Theater of the Galaxies Clue: with all my heart
Row, Row, Row Your Boat Cross the "water" and gather balloons. **Walk on Water Dash** Dash across the water without getting wet.	Peach Boat or Boats-a-Float	"All Things Are Possible" (Praise Music and Video) Water Moon Boot Scoot or Mission Possible (Key Verse Memory Activities)	Water's Ups and Downs A change in air pressure causes water to amazingly rise inside a jar, teaching that we can trust God even when things seem impossible.	Location: SuperNova SuperMart Clue: I will tell
Pass It On Form a cross using tape, streamers, and balloons. **Criss-Cross** Work as a team to build a cross.	Berry Blastoff or Resurrection Butterflies	"God of Power" (Praise Music and Video) Resurrection Roll or Docking Station (Key Verse Memory Activities)	Inflatable Power A common white powder sets off an effervescent reaction, providing kids with an illustration of the resurrection power that they can talk about with others.	Location: Wonder U. Clue: of all your wonders

Exploration Expectations for Leaders

So, are you ready to blast off into a spectacular adventure of faith with *Cosmic City*™ VBS? Your role as the Games Director is a pivotal part of the vacation Bible school experience for the Space Voyagers on tour this week. By participating and having fun with the games you'll be coordinating, kids will apply the theme to their lives in an age-appropriate way.

They're coming to you for fun and activity. So what exactly do you need to do?

SEVERAL MONTHS BEFORE VBS:

✶ Read each day's Bible story and the "Bible Story Summaries" section. Instead of relying on your familiarity with the story, take some time to explore the Scripture passage with fresh eyes. Ask yourself: What will God teach *me* through this story? What are the most important truths here? How can I communicate God's message to the kids?

✶ Thoroughly read each day's games.

✶ Locate supplies you'll need for the games (or recruit someone who can help you with this task).

A FEW WEEKS BEFORE VBS:

✶ Learn how the games run.

✶ Practice the games with some of your helpers.

✶ Decorate your room (the week before VBS). Enlist help, since it only makes the task more enjoyable!

THE WEEK OF VBS:

✶ Pray together with your games volunteers, asking God to help you communicate the truths of his Word through the games.

✶ Talk with Tour Hosts (adults) and Guides (teens) about any help you'll need from them during each day's games. Make sure they're ready to participate enthusiastically.

✶ Constantly encourage and support your volunteers.

✶ Stay sensitive to the Holy Spirit. Watch your kids to see where God might be working and help him make an impact. Through it all, have fun!

POST-VBS:

✶ Enlist help to dismantle decorations and props. Store any you think you might use again.

✶ Send thank you notes, or even host a party, to show appreciation for your volunteers.

✶ Follow up with the children as appropriate, along with your Tour Director and other VBS leaders.

See? It's not going to be that hard! You'll have a blast facilitating out-of-this-world fun!

QUICK TIP!

You'll want to have a minimum of one consistent helper per every ten kids that visit your station. Ask your Tour Director for the approximate number of kids each group will contain.

Cosmic Clue Quest

As children tour Cosmic City, they'll experience countless moments filled with fun, excitement, and the awe and wonder of God. And just when they think they've discovered everything the city has to offer, they'll stumble across a quest more adventurous than any other: the Cosmic Clue Quest. During each day's tour, Space Voyagers will search for the Cosmic Clue at a different tour stop.

The Cosmic Clue Quest will take place at Asteroid Alley on Day 2. On this day, print each word of your clue, taken from Psalm 9:1, on a separate slip of paper (see below). Then hide each slip throughout your space, marking its spot with a star. (You can cut stars out of construction paper, approximately two inches from end to end, or use standard star stickers.)

When children arrive at your tour stop on Day 2, encourage them to find the clues by looking for the stars. When all the clues are located, work as a group to unscramble them. Then have children open their *Student Books* to page 10 and write the clues on the appropriate lines.

COSMIC CLUES

Day 1—Deeper Space: I will praise you
Day 2—Asteroid Alley: O Lord
Day 3—The Theater of the Galaxies: with all my heart
Day 4—SuperNova SuperMart: I will tell
Day 5—Wonder U.: of all your wonders

Have a stellar quest!

Decorating Your Universe—Setup and Décor

Welcome your Space Voyagers to Asteroid Alley with some out-of-this-world decorations. Grab their attention and get them all fired up for a cosmic journey into fun and games. Here are a few suggestions to help in creating a truly cosmic atmosphere!

✴ Welcome the Space Voyagers by displaying the large Asteroid Alley sign above the door, available for order at www.cookvbs.com. You can even attach the sign to a post and stick it in the ground if your Asteroid Alley tour stop is outside.

✴ Hang planets from the ceiling. If your Asteroid Alley is located indoors, hang colorful planets to make your tour stop fun and space-like. You can purchase decorative planets at a local teacher store or create your own using large Styrofoam balls that you paint to resemble different planets in our solar system, or even imaginative planets from galaxies far away.

✴ Make large asteroids. Use very large trash bags, and fill them with crumpled up newspaper. Tie the trash bags closed to make the asteroids. (You may want to paint the trash bags with various shades of brown, grey, and black to give them a more realistic look.) If your Asteroid Alley is located indoors, hang some asteroids from the ceiling using heavy string. Number other asteroids by taping numbered sheets of copy paper on them. Set these asteroids on the ground.

✴ Set up a table and decorate it using a space tablecloth for a "blastoff table." Or, you can cover the table with white paper. Color cosmic creations on it and use the table to keep all of the game items needed, plus some extras.

✴ Use blue, grey, black, or silver streamers to add flair to the game area for "space streamers" if your Asteroid Alley is located indoors. You might wish to hang the streamers creating an alley through which the children enter the game area.

✴ Cut large sheets of paper into different shapes such as rockets, moon, sun, and stars for posters. Provide markers and have the children color cosmic creations on each one. Tape the posters to the wall.

✴ Blow up large balloons for "blastoff balloons." Tape balloons together in a row, then form an archway or alley through which the children enter. Use a large black permanent marker to write a letter on each balloon to create the words, "Asteroid Alley."

✴ Use rope lights or mini string lights and attach them to ceilings, walls, or tables for a cosmic lights effect. Go crazy with lights!

✴ Cut out large, circular shapes from cardboard to make flying saucers. Cover one side of the cardboard with foil. Attach mini string lights to the foiled side of the cardboard. Use the lights to form a circular pattern starting the pattern in the middle and winding your way out. Hang the flying saucer on the wall or from the ceiling and light it up.

Outdoor Options

✴ Weight the trash bag asteroids by placing sand in the bottom of each trash bag, preventing them from blowing in the wind. Use these asteroids as markers instead of cones for areas where games are to be played.

✴ Hang streamers from trees or the edge of a building.

✴ Cut large sheets of cardboard into different shapes such as rockets, moon, sun, and stars for posters. Provide markers and have the children color cosmic creations on each one. Set the posters on easels or up against a building or some rocks.

✴ Blow up large balloons for "blastoff balloons." Tape balloons together in a row and attach them to a wire trellis to form an archway or alley through which the children enter.

✴ Cut out large circular shapes from cardboard to make flying saucers. Hang the flying saucers from a tree or the end of a building.

Space Guide—Teacher Tips

QUICK TIP!

Use a device such as a whistle, your hands (clap), or a horn to get your group's attention. When the children hear the sound, they respond with an action. A simple and fun sound and action response could be a pattern blown on a whistle or clapped out to the rhythm of "long, short, short, short, long … pause." All of the children then respond by shouting, "Blast Off" and putting their hands together over their heads to form a rocket. Practice the sound and action response with the children. Be sure they understand that everyone freezes and is quiet after they shout, "Blast Off" and form their rockets.

Welcome to Asteroid Alley, where you're sure to be bombarded with fun and games! In this guide, you'll find everything you need to know in order to successfully lead your children every day in original, thematic *Cosmic City™* games. Each day you're given two game options to choose from. You'll find that each day's Option 1 game usually requires a higher activity level from the children and more prep time on your part. You'll find Option 2 games to be slightly lower-key but every bit as challenging and fun as the first options. Each game in this manual is designed for playing in a large open area, either indoors or outdoors.

Here are a few general tips for game leaders:

GET KIDS' ATTENTION TO GATHER THEM IN A GROUP, TO GIVE INSTRUCTION, OR TO STOP PLAY.

A really effective way to get their attention—especially if the noise level is loud or children are spread out in a playing area—is to use a sound and action response.

ORGANIZE AND PREPARE. BRING YOUR BIBLE.

Always plan for more children than you expect. Lay things out, and prepare in advance. Always plan to fill more time than you are allotted. And always be ready for unseen circumstances such as wind, rain, space limitations, and missing or broken items. Don't forget! Bring your Bible each day of VBS. Have children watch you reading and referring to it for the day's Bible story before and after play.

USE THE PEOPLE WHO HAVE BEEN ASSIGNED TO HELP.

Don't assume they'll know what to do. It's usually helpful to make an, "I need …" statement when delegating responsibility or delivering expectations.

GIVE SPECIFIC INSTRUCTIONS.

Point things out to the children such as start and finish lines, boundaries, and equipment. Give instructions a chunk at a time. Then select a Space Voyager to restate the instructions. After giving the instructions, give a brief overview of the whole game and the main goal of the game. Always ask if anyone has any questions before beginning a game.

DEMONSTRATE WHAT YOU NEED WHEN GIVING INSTRUCTIONS.

Most kids learn best by observing and watching, and then by doing. Make sure that you emphasize and demonstrate the right way to do things. It's also helpful in some cases to demonstrate the wrong way to do something. In those cases, make sure to follow up with another example of the right way to do it. Use a Guide or Tour Host to help demonstrate.

ENCOURAGE THE CHILDREN TO PARTICIPATE AND NOT TO GIVE UP DURING PLAY.

Engage children during instruction by asking them to demonstrate how the game is played. During play, encourage those who seem frustrated or discouraged by affirming what they're doing well.

CONNECT WITH YOUR SPACE VOYAGERS.

Really get to know your children. Take time to ask questions about their families, pets, school, and friends. Let them get to know you too.

SHOW YOUR ENTHUSIASM AND GET CRAZY!

If you're excited to learn about God, it will become infectious and the children will ooze with it too!

WATCH FOR SPACE VOYAGERS WHO ARE FOLLOWING THE RULES AND THOSE WHO ARE NOT.

Point out the positive, and celebrate with the whole group the children who are following the rules. Be specific as to what the child is doing to follow the rules. For example: "Way to go, Cody! You're doing a great job by gently tagging the other team players. Thanks for making this a fun and safe game."

GIVE CHOICES WHEN WORKING WITH SPACE VOYAGERS WHO MIGHT BE A LITTLE CHALLENGING.

Pull the child aside, use eye contact, and use the child's name when talking with him or her. For example: "Olivia, I saw that you threw that bean bag much too hard. When playing this game, you only need to toss it. Olivia, you have a choice: you can continue to play the game by tossing the bean bag appropriately, or you can sit out of the game. Which do you choose?" If Olivia is really stubborn, then you can respond with, "I'll give you to the count of three to choose or I'll choose for you." If she still doesn't choose, then make a choice for her.

GIVE SPACE VOYAGERS TIME TO PARTICIPATE.

Some Space Voyagers might not want to jump right into an activity. This is normal for some children. Many children need time to observe the rules, how a game is played, or how people respond during an activity. Once they've had a chance to observe the game, ask if they wish to join the group.

Blast off for a great time!

QUICK TIP!

Crazy and goofy fun can make a few children feel uncomfortable or out of control. If this happens, approach the child and ask what he or she needs. Most of the time children know what they need in order to feel comfortable.

QUICK TIP!

For those who don't follow the rules, pull them aside individually. Quietly state what he or she is doing wrong. Then talk about what should be done, and give the Voyager an opportunity to show you how to do it right. He or she might need a little extra practice by demonstrating to you how it can be done right on the sidelines, before joining the group.

Voyage Essentials—Master Supply List

DAY 1

Option 1: Creation Stations
- [ ] 7 chairs
- [ ] 7 sheets of paper
- [ ] Tape
- [ ] 19 index cards
- [ ] Markers

Option 2: String Creations
- [ ] Heavy string, yarn, or rope
- [ ] 12 index cards

DAY 2

Option 1: Manna Madness
- [ ] 100 index cards
- [ ] 2 small shoe boxes without lids
- [ ] Masking tape
- [ ] Safety cones
- [ ] 2 chairs

Option 2: Birds and Bread Blastoff
- [ ] Small craft feathers, one per child
- [ ] Cotton balls
- [ ] Sandwich bags, one per child
- [ ] Timer

DAY 3

Option 1: Mat Mix-up
- [ ] 4 small carpet squares (2' x 3') or welcome mats or bath towels
- [ ] 4 chairs
- [ ] 4 clean long socks
- [ ] Masking tape/cones

Option 2: Mega Mats
- [ ] 30-gallon yard and leaf trash bags, one per team
- [ ] Masking tape
- [ ] Scissors

DAY 4

Option 1: Row, Row, Row Your Boat
- [ ] Masking tape
- [ ] Plastic play hoops, one per team
- [ ] Small tarp (8' x 10')
- [ ] 40 balloons
- [ ] Spray water bottles

Option 2: Walk on Water Dash
- [ ] Masking tape
- [ ] 2 buckets of water
- [ ] 10 small sponges
- [ ] 20 large paper grocery bags

DAY 5

Option 1: Pass It On
- [ ] 10-14 balloons per team
- [ ] Small tarp (8' x 10')
- [ ] Rolls of masking tape, one per team
- [ ] Rolls of streamers, one per team
- [ ] Optional: large trash bags

Option 2: Criss-cross
- [ ] 22 large foam cups per team
- [ ] 2 beach towels per team

Cosmic Caring—Special Learners

IT'S A WIDE SPECTRUM

Kids learn in all sorts of ways—through words, music, movement, art, introspection, and so on. *Cosmic City*™ VBS offers a range of learning activities that will touch kids in all these areas. But some kids will still need an extra dose of understanding because their development differs from other kids their age. They may simply need some extra time and encouragement, or they may have a special need that's mental, physical, or behavioral in nature.

ORDER IN CHAOS

Accepting special learners in your class doesn't mean giving in to chaos. All kids need structure and predictability. Use these suggestions to make special learners comfortable, and encourage appropriate participation as much as possible.

1. Adapt the way everyone does the activity. Make adjustments that include the special learner and still accomplish the point of the activity. For example, if an activity calls for children to pass a squishy ball around the circle to the beat of the music, but you know Miranda will want to hold on to it, give everyone a ball made of wadded paper. Have each child pass his wad from one hand to the other, still to the beat of the music.

2. Arrange for extra help. Take advantage of Cosmic City's teen Guides. A child like Zack may need someone to be his buddy with gentle reminders of appropriate behavior. Sometimes just the presence of another adult or teen in the group helps all the kids stay within the right parameters.

3. Allow for variety. Not everyone has to do everything the same way. If Lynette wants to color her craft on the floor while everyone else paints at a table, so what? You're after participation and learning, not a battle for dominance.

4. Adopt new habits. Give warnings about transitions, clarify instructions, set supplies out ahead of time, touch a shoulder and smile, or make a point to speak a word of encouragement to a struggling child. Teaching children isn't as much about getting through the material as it is making connections that keep you in touch with what they're learning.

5. Adjust your attitude. Let's face it—some kids can be frustrating. You may even find yourself secretly hoping rambunctious Travis doesn't come tomorrow. But remember the attitude of Jesus, a sacrificial, humble servant who gave up the honor he deserved.

QUICK TIP!
Be so prepared on the first day that when kids arrive you can focus on them. Observe them and take note of insecurities or challenges you see so that you can address them throughout the week.

QUICK TIP!
Just as children with special needs have unique styles of learning, so do gifted and advanced learners. Keep in mind that some children may appear bored or even become disruptive when they master a concept or activity more quickly than the others. Engage these advanced learners by giving them opportunities to help their classmates or to create challenging additions to the activity.

QUICK TIP!
If you're struggling to connect with a special learner, try looking inward. What is it about your own personality or background that may be contributing to difficult times?

Mission Command—Leading a Child to Christ

It's amazing how often adult Christians say that they first came to understand the unfolding of God's story when they were between six and twelve years old. These years are a key time for children to make personal decisions for Christ and to begin their faith journeys. *Cosmic City*™ VBS may be the experience that makes a child think about expressing faith in Christ and receiving God's saving grace.

Keep in mind that no two children are at the same point of spiritual preparedness. Many children aren't ready to trust in Christ even at the upper end of elementary school; other children can be quite sincere in saying they want Jesus to be their Savior even as preschoolers. They're sensitive to their need for forgiveness and acceptance into God's family. Be open to the Holy Spirit's leading. Be available to answer questions, but let children decide when the time is right to receive Christ. Here are a few tips:

✶ Be careful not to let your eagerness spur children to make a faith decision, since VBS is a time when our radar is eagerly seeking kids who are ready to trust Christ for salvation. Kids will pick up on what will make the teacher happy and perhaps say they want to make a decision when the truth is they don't yet understand what they're saying.

✶ Look for opportunities to invite children to receive Christ individually, rather than just making group invitations. Kids are great conformists; they may respond to such an invitation just because everyone else is doing it. Encourage children to talk privately with you about questions regarding salvation and what Jesus wants to do in their lives, and then be sure you're available for these conversations.

✶ Have the child tell you in his or her own words what he or she wants. If you feel the child understands the concept of salvation and is ready to receive Christ by faith, take a few minutes to pray with him or her. You and the child will want to talk with parents about this decision. Parents who don't attend church may have questions about salvation, and this opens the door for you to witness to them and invite them to your church.

✶ Remember your important ministry of follow-up. Pray for the child and encourage discipleship and Christian growth. Send a personal note—kids love to get mail addressed to them!

EXPLAINING SALVATION

The following suggestions may be helpful as you explain the message of salvation. Help the child know the truths that are fundamental for all Christians. Ask your Tour Director for some copies of the reproducible on page 18 of the *Director's Guide*. It will help the child follow these important steps and give him something to take home as a reminder of his decision.

Step 1: God loves us even though we sin (Rom. 5:8). We must recognize that we deserve God's punishment, and his love is a free gift (Rom. 6:23).

Step 2: Even though God loves us, our sin separates us from him. But he wants to forgive us, and he will if we ask (1 John 1:9).

Step 3: Believing in Jesus and inviting him to lead your life is the way to accept God's forgiveness (Rom. 10:9–10). Jesus is God's perfect Son, and he died on a cross to take the consequences of our sin (John 3:16).

Mission Command—Leading a Child to Christ, continued

Jesus didn't stay dead. God brought him back to life to prove he's stronger than our sin. Because Jesus died and rose again, God can forgive us.

Step 4: Once we ask for God's forgiveness, we can celebrate because we're sure he forgives us (1 John 1:9). Now we're part of God's family forever (John 1:12), and we want to learn as much about him as we can. Reading the Bible, praying, and worshipping are some ways we learn more about him (2 Peter 3:18).

Step 5: When we have the good news of being in God's family (John 1:12), we want to tell others about it (Matt. 10:32; 28:19). Encourage children to express their decisions in their own words. Clarify any confusion.

During your conversation, you may want to share some additional verses with the child. The verses below might help. Read them from a Bible, not just the page. You don't have to use them all in every conversation. Different verses may answer the questions of individual children.

✶ John 1:12—"Yet to all who received him, to those who believed in his name, he gave the right to become children of God."

✶ John 3:16—"For God so loved the world that he gave his one and only Son, that whoever believes in him shall not perish but have eternal life."

✶ Romans 3:23—"For all have sinned and fall short of the glory of God."

✶ Romans 5:8—"But God demonstrates his own love for us in this: While we were still sinners, Christ died for us."

✶ Romans 6:23—"For the wages of sin is death, but the gift of God is eternal life in Christ Jesus our Lord."

✶ Romans 10:9–10—"If you confess with your mouth, 'Jesus is Lord,' and believe in your heart that God raised him from the dead, you will be saved. For it is with your heart that you believe and are justified, and it is with your mouth that you confess and are saved."

✶ 2 Corinthians 5:17—"Therefore, if anyone is in Christ, he is a new creation; the old has gone, the new has come!"

✶ 1 John 5:11–12—"And this is the testimony: God has given us eternal life, and this life is in his Son. He who has the Son has life; he who does not have the Son of God does not have life."

Abridged Travel Manual—Bible Story Summaries

Day 1—God's Wondrous Creation

BIBLE STORY

God's Wondrous Creation (Gen. 1:1—2:4; Ps. 136:1–9, 25–26)

KEY VERSE

Before the mountains were born or you brought forth the earth and the world, from everlasting to everlasting you are God. (Ps. 90:2)

LIVE IT!

God is awesome! I can worship him.

A LITTLE BACKGROUND...

Today's Bible story explores the fantastic cosmic fireworks display that starts the Bible: God's creation of the world. And though the creation account is awesome on its own, it also points us to an important reality for all people of faith, both young and old alike. The apostle Paul explains in Romans 1:20, "Since the creation of the world God's invisible qualities—his eternal power and divine nature—have been clearly seen, being understood from what has been made."

We can see God's power through his amazing act of creation recorded in Genesis, and evidence of his reality and character by simply taking a look at the world he created.

Even a few moments spent contemplating God's amazing world inspires awe and wonder. Brilliant sunsets render us speechless. Sparkling stars on a quiet night trigger thoughts beyond earthly matters. The melodies of birds on a peaceful morning delight the soul. Even the thunder, lightning, and rhythmic sounds of a stormy night remind us how small we are in the grand scheme of life. More than anything, such occasions offer a brief glimpse of God's incredible majesty—a majesty praised by the elders in Revelation 4:11, "You are worthy, our Lord and God, to receive glory and honor and power, for you created all things, and by your will they were created and have their being."

God's incredible creation naturally fascinates and inspires children. By looking at the world they can begin to understand the God who made it and find their hearts worshipping him in response. Everything around them can become infused with great meaning and spiritual truth.

Today's exploration of the creation account points kids beyond simply *what* was created to *who* created it. As they participate today, children will discover important aspects of who God is: God is a creative artist, God is loving, God is powerful, God is personal, and God is *real*. And we can worship him!

Day 2—Desert Wonder

A LITTLE BACKGROUND...

Today's Bible story includes some serious complainers: a bunch of Israelites with bad attitudes wandering in the desert. It's easy to point a finger at them—but if we're honest, we have to admit that we often do the same thing! How many of us would be able to walk day after day through a blistering hot desert without complaining? Despite God's amazing provision in our lives, we often take for granted the truth that we can count on him, and instead fixate on all the parts of our lives that seem to be going wrong.

The events of Exodus 16 and 17 are set against the backdrop of some of the most amazing events in Old Testament history. God called Moses through a burning bush, Moses powerfully confronted Pharaoh, God afflicted Egypt with plagues, the Israelites were freed, God parted the Red Sea, and through God's power the ferocious Egyptian army was annihilated. Talk about *awesome!* A display of power like this would be hard to forget; yet, sadly, the Israelites are quick to put this miraculous past behind them and find reasons not to trust God as they plod through the desert. It was only human for them to wonder, "If God loves us, then why is he making things so *hard* for us?"

Deuteronomy 8:3 tells us that God had a reason for the hunger and thirst he allowed the Israelites to experience during their desert wanderings: "He humbled you, causing you to hunger and then feeding you with manna ... to teach you that man does not live on bread alone but on every word that comes from the mouth of the LORD." God's purpose in providing manna, quail, and water was not just to meet the Israelites' physical needs—his intention was to show them that God himself is the perfect Provision they needed ... and *we* need. God is our manna—our bread. Jesus alluded to this same concept when he said, "I am the bread of life. He who comes to me will never go hungry, and he who believes in me will never be thirsty" (John 6:35).

It's in a relationship with God through faith in Jesus that our deepest hunger is fulfilled and our thirst is quenched. Through God's provision for the Israelites, kids can discover that God is trustworthy and they can count on him—not only for practical needs in their lives, but also as the true sustenance for their souls.

Day 3—Healing Wonder

A LITTLE BACKGROUND...

On the surface, the events of Luke 5:17–26 are stunningly spectacular. Some men, passionate about getting their friend to Jesus to be healed, don't let anything get in their way—not even a crowd of people or the roof of a house. They dig, cut, and rip

---

BIBLE STORY

God Provided Manna, Quail, and Water for the Israelites (Exod. 16:1–17, 31–36; 17:1–6)

KEY VERSE

The LORD will guide you always; he will satisfy your needs. (Is. 58:11)

LIVE IT!

God is awesome! I can count on him.

BIBLE STORY

Jesus Heals a Paralyzed Man (Luke 5:17–26)

KEY VERSE

You are the God who performs miracles; you display your power among the peoples. (Ps. 77:14)

LIVE IT!

God is awesome! I can believe in him.

their way through the roof in order to lower their paralyzed friend to the ground in front of Jesus. Then they wait in expectation. Will their hopes be answered? Will their friend be healed?

Jesus *does* heal their friend, and in quite a dramatic fashion. One minute, the man is motionless on a mat; the next, he's holding his mat under his arm and *walking* home praising God. Wow!

But there's a hidden thread in this story that's even more awe-inspiring than the physical healing that takes place. It's the profound healing power of Jesus' *words* that are the true miracle in this account. Jesus tells the paralytic, "Friend, your sins are forgiven."

Not only does Jesus provide outward, physical healing, but he also addresses the inner need of the paralytic and reveals himself as the true healer of humankind. Jesus uses this metaphor of physical healing to explain his reason for befriending sinners in Matthew 9:12, saying, "It is not the healthy who need a doctor, but the sick." Jesus, the Son of God, has the power to heal us of our deepest wound: our separation from God as a result of our sin.

Jesus' statement to the paralytic is profound not only for the forgiveness he offers, but also for the word "friend." It's in this kind first word Jesus speaks to the paralyzed man that we get a glimpse of the type of relationship God desires to have with us. Jesus calls the man not into a cold, distant religion with a remote, uncaring deity, but into an intimate *friendship* with the loving God who has forgiven him.

Today's lesson will allow children to share in the excitement of the men who brought their friend to Jesus and witnessed the miracle that happened that day. But beyond the events of the story, they'll learn the exciting truth that Jesus can heal *them* too. They can find this healing in the forgiveness of sins he offers and the friend relationship they can have with him through faith.

Day 4—Water Wonder

A LITTLE BACKGROUND...

It could be argued that all the disciples who were in the boat the night Matthew writes about in chapter 14 "trusted" Jesus. After all, many had made major sacrifices to become his follower, leaving their families and careers behind to travel from village to village. And they'd all just witnessed a fantastic miracle—Jesus had used five loaves of bread and two fish to feed over 5,000 people! Talk about a trust-booster!

That night, they *all* saw Jesus walking toward them on the water. But only *one* disciple, Peter, trusted Jesus enough to swing his leg over the side, place his foot on the water, and step out to Jesus.

For a moment, try to wipe away your familiarity with this story and see it with a fresh perspective. This was a real man doing something completely insane—hefting his

BIBLE STORY
Jesus Walks on Water
(Matt.14:22–33)

KEY VERSE
All things are possible with God.
(Mark 10:27)

LIVE IT!
God is awesome! I can trust him.

body onto liquid H_2O. If you were there, would *you* have done that?

As we all know, the story doesn't end there. When Peter felt the rain pelting his face, heard the wind howling in his ears, saw the waves tossing about all around him, he was afraid and immediately began to sink. But Jesus saved Peter and challenged his faith, asking, "Why did you doubt?"

So, is the point of this story for us to berate Peter for his doubt and his lack of trust? Are we to hold Peter up as an example of a person with small faith, teaching kids to focus on Peter's failure?

Or instead, can we look at the story through a different lens? Step back from that scene of Jesus clutching Peter, pulling him up out of the waves, and focus in on the boat Peter left behind. That boat is full of Jesus-followers who *didn't* step out onto the water.

Clearly Peter still had growing to do, and the Gospels record many similar interactions between Jesus and Peter in which Jesus uses Peter's faults and failings to teach him about true faith (Matt. 16:21–28; 26:31–35, 69–75; John 21:15–19). But Peter's willingness to throw caution to the wind (literally) and step out onto the water is a powerful example we can use to show children what it means to truly trust Jesus.

We see another bold step from Peter just two chapters later, when he's the first disciple to courageously declare, "You are the Christ, the Son of the living God" (Matt. 16: 16). Peter shows us that trusting Jesus isn't merely a mental assent or a casual relationship; it's not a safe faith that clings to the comfort and security of a familiar boat. It's a trust that steps out into the water—it's a risky, bold, whole-person response of complete commitment to Jesus. It's a trust that puts it all on the line in response to Jesus' call.

As you explore today's **Live It!** point with the kids, you can use the activities to help them see that they can *trust* Jesus to help them make it through the various challenging circumstances that come their way. But even more importantly, they can trust Jesus with their lives; they can believe in him with all their hearts, commit everything to him, and make him the Lord of their lives.

Day 5—The Wonder of God Brought Down to Earth

A LITTLE BACKGROUND...

Today's lesson introduces children to the meaning of the resurrection and the real reason it's so spectacular. It's not simply the miracle of a dead man coming back to life. It's the miracle of the defeat of sin and death, the miracle of forgiveness and eternity with God being offered to us undeserving humans. This isn't the ho-hum news or the so-so news—this is the *good* news! It's the best news ever, and it's worth celebrating.

This news is also worth *sharing*. When Jesus gave the Great Commission in Matthew 28:19–20, he didn't say, "And when you reach age eighteen, go and make

BIBLE STORY

Jesus' Resurrection (John 19:1–6, 16–18; 20:1–8)

KEY VERSE

I want to know Christ and the power of his resurrection. (Philippians 3:10)

LIVE IT!

God is awesome! I can tell others about Jesus.

disciples…" Jesus' kingdom includes its youngest citizens and his commission applies to them as well. Jesus commended the trusting, honest, open, and sincere faith of children (Matt. 18:3 and 19:14). And the truth of the matter is, kids can sometimes do an even *better* job than adults at sharing their faith! As they reach out to their friends and playmates by sharing Jesus with them or inviting them to church functions like Sunday school, a midweek program, or VBS, they have the ability to plant seeds of faith. Today, as Space Voyagers get a closer look at Mary, Peter, and John's excitement about telling others the good news, watch *them* get excited about their own mission. They too can share the "awesome news" about the best day ever seen on planet Earth.

God's Wondrous Creation

BIBLE STORY
God's Wondrous Creation (Gen.1:1—2:4; Ps. 136:1–9, 25–26)

KEY VERSE
Before the mountains were born or you brought forth the earth and the world, from everlasting to everlasting you are God. (Ps. 90:2)

LIVE IT! God is awesome! I can worship him.

SUPPLIES
* 7 chairs
* 7 sheets of paper
* Tape
* 19 index cards
* Markers
* Bible

PREP TIME
15 minutes

FIELD TEST TIP
Since the first couple of groups that visit your site will not have heard the Bible story in Theater of the Galaxies, you'll want to emphasize the Bible story and **Live It!** when children arrive.

Game Option 1: Creation Stations

GOAL
Reinforce today's Bible story with visits to seven Creation Stations.

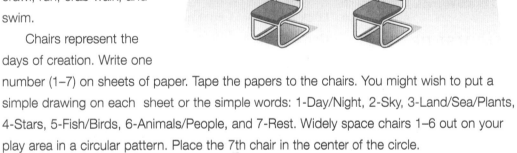

DO AHEAD
Number two sets of index cards 1–7. Shuffle. Use the remaining 5 cards to create a separate deck of movement cards. Write one of the following action words on each card: hop, crawl, run, crab walk, and swim.

Chairs represent the days of creation. Write one number (1–7) on sheets of paper. Tape the papers to the chairs. You might wish to put a simple drawing on each sheet or the simple words: 1-Day/Night, 2-Sky, 3-Land/Sea/Plants, 4-Stars, 5-Fish/Birds, 6-Animals/People, and 7-Rest. Widely space chairs 1–6 out on your play area in a circular pattern. Place the 7th chair in the center of the circle.

Ready, Set, Blast Off!

FIELD TEST TIP

Space the chairs further apart for more challenging play. And to increase the fun—call out a creation day and point to the wrong chair. See how long it takes for kids to catch on! The faster you call out the stations, the crazier the game gets!

Launch Farther!

Bring Asteroid Alley to life by becoming a resident of Cosmic City™ for the week! Dress and act the part of a Cosmic City™ Coach. Wear a whistle around your neck, dress in athletic shorts or pants, and ask children to refer to you as "Coach (your name)." You may even want to refer to the Tour Guides as "Assistant Coaches." Bring your own ideas and creativity into your character; just be sure you're consistent throughout all five days.

FIELD TEST TIP

Have both games prepared for play each day. Two games will fill the time nicely for smaller groups.

FIELD TEST TIP

Have older kids read portions of today's Creation story (Gen.1:1—2:4; Ps. 136:1–9, 25–26) from your Bible before and after play to reinforce the awesome power of God's Word.

Who created the world? (Pause, allowing children to think about the question and answer it aloud if they choose.) **How do we know God created the world?** (Pause.) **In the Bible the book of Genesis says God created everything. It says that at first there was nothing and it was dark; there was only God. God has always been from the very beginning before anything else was created. God is eternal.**

On the first day of creation, God created light. God continued with six more days of creation. There were seven days of creation in all. God created the sky, the land, the seas, and the plants. Then God created all of the stars in the sky. After that God created the fish and the birds. God had created so many wonderful things, but he wasn't finished yet. God continued and created the animals. The very last thing God created was the most amazing—God created people. Finally on the seventh day, God rested. God is an awesome God. The Bible tells us that God created the universe, the world, and everything in it. Have the children repeat the **Live It!** statement with you: **God is awesome! I can worship him.**

Look around and you'll see seven Creation Station chairs. Each station chair represents one of the days of God's wondrous creation. I'll call out an action or movement. You'll have to do this movement to get to the Creation Station. For example, let's say I call out "hop." Pause for a moment, allowing children to practice hopping in place. **Now I'll call out a station.** Call out, **"Creation Station, Day 2." Everyone must hop to the Creation Station that represents Day 2. Let's give it a try.** Once everyone arrives at Day 2, draw a card for a new movement and another card for a new Creation Station.

Announce the movement and get the kids ready. Then announce, **Creation Station, Day ___!** Continue to shuffle cards and draw new ones. Play as time allows.

Re-entry: Questions That Bring It Home

★ Look around you right now. Name three amazing things (or people) that God created.

★ If you could have watched one day of creation as it happened, which would you choose? Why?

★ We were each created in the image, or likeness, of God. And each of us has the ability to be creative. What's your favorite thing to create, or invent? (For example, drawings, games, songs, etc.)

Game Option 2: String Creations

DO AHEAD
Write one of the following words on separate index cards: sun, half-moon, star, flower, fish, leaf, mountain, horse, snake, tree, rock, and person.

Cut string. (String length will vary depending on the size of your group. The larger the group, the longer the string should be. A good estimate is about 2 yards of string per child. For the recommended group size of five children, you will need 10 yards of string). Tie the ends of the string together.

Ready, Set, Blast Off!

Divide the children into teams of five. Give each team one piece of string. Have each team form a circle, pulling on the string to create one large string circle. Be sure each child holds on tight to the string during play. When it's time to begin the activity, have children step toward the center of their group forming a tight circle; the string will be loose between them.

The Bible tells us that in the beginning, there was only God. Can you imagine ... only God ... nothing else existed. There was no sun, no moon, no Earth, no plants, no animals, and no people. But God created everything. God took six days to create the stars, sun, moon, Earth, sky, oceans, plants, animals, and even people. On the seventh day God rested. God is so amazing and so powerful. How awesome is a God who can create everything out of nothing? Have the children repeat the **Live It!** statement with you: **God is awesome! I can worship him.**

Launch Farther!
This game can be played as an activity or as a competition. If played as a competition, judge the winning groups based on different criteria, such as fastest group, most creative group, best teamwork, and best creations. Let children use whatever it takes—their feet, elbows, or heads—to make their creations. Just be sure you encourage them to always hang on to the string!

At the end of each game you'll find a set of discussion questions called "Re-entry." These questions help children make practical connections between the game and the day's Bible lesson. If time allows, ask these questions to the whole group or have kids discuss them in small groups or with partners.

We're going to play a game. As a group you'll try to make string creations. I'll tell you what to make using your string. The creations you'll be making will remind us of what God created. I'll say, "God's wondrous _____ creation." I'm going to fill in the blank with a word from these cards. Show the group the cards. As a group, you'll work together to create the object using your string. Remember not to let go of your spot on the string. Let's give it a try.

Draw one of the cards. Shout out the phrase, filling in the blank with the object they're to create using their strings. Continue to draw different cards and shout out the phrase with the different items they're to create.

Re-entry: Questions That Bring It Home

* Look around you right now. Name three amazing things (or people) that God created.
* If you could have watched one day of creation as it happened, which would you choose? Why?
* We were each created in the image, or likeness, of God. And each of us has the ability to be creative. What's your favorite thing to create, or invent? (For example, drawings, games, songs, etc.)

Desert Wonder

BIBLE STORY
God Provided Manna, Quail, and Water for the Israelites (Ex. 16:1–17, 31–36; 17:1–6)

KEY VERSE
The LORD will guide you always; he will satisfy your needs. (Isa. 58:11)

LIVE IT! God is awesome! I can count on him.

SUPPLIES
* 100 index cards
* 2 small shoe boxes (without lids)
* Masking tape
* Safety cones
* 2 chairs
* Bible

PREP TIME
15 minutes

The Global Positioning System, or GPS, consists of 24 satellites launched into orbit by the U.S. Department of Defense. GPS works in any weather, anywhere in the world, 24 hours a day.[2]

Game Option 1: Manna Madness

GOAL
Collect "manna" without getting tagged by the opposing team.

DO AHEAD
Use cones to mark off a large rectangular play area—the larger the better. Use masking tape, rope or spray paint (if on grass) to divide the area in half. Place a chair in the center of each half. Place a shoe box on each chair. Use scissors to round off the edges of 50 of the index cards. Leave the other cards rectangular. As the diagram below suggests, spread out the oval manna cards on one side of the playing area and the rectangular manna cards on the other half.

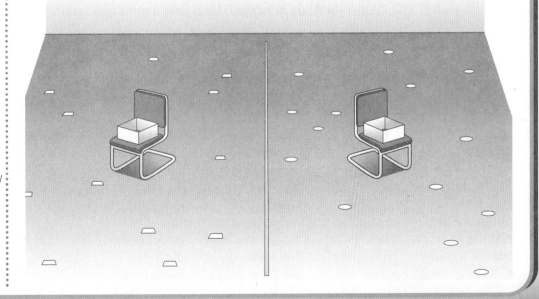

Ready, Set, Blast Off!

The Israelites were in a tough spot. They were living in the desert, and they were tired, extremely thirsty, and very hungry. In fact, they were starving! Where would their next meal come from? Their next meal came from an awesome God. God heard their cries and answered their prayers. God provided manna, bread from heaven, for the people to eat. In the morning when the people would awake, the manna would be on the ground. The people would collect the manna. By night God sent birds called quail. The people would gather the quail so they would have meat to eat. The Israelites counted on God for their food and water. God is awesome, and we can count on him too. Have the children repeat the **Live It!** statement with you: **God is awesome! I can count on him.**

Let's play a game where we collect manna. It'll remind us of how God provided for the Israelites.

Separate the children into two teams. Have each team sit on opposite sides of the playing area. **Let's get started. Each team has a manna gathering box.** Point to the box on each chair. **Your job will be to pick up manna, and put it in your team's box. The team who picks up all of their manna first wins. Sounds easy, right? Well, here's the madness part!** Motion to the team sitting on the side of the playing area with the oval manna. **You're Team A. Team A may only collect manna that's *rectangular*.** Motion to the team sitting on the side of the playing area with the rectangular manna. **Team B, you may only collect *oval* manna. In other words, both teams will have to cross to the other side of the playing area to get their manna.**

Pick up a piece of manna. **Here are the rules of play:**

1) **Pick up only one piece of manna at a time.**
2) **The opposing team will try and tag you if you're on their side and have a piece of manna in your hand.**
3) **If you're tagged, drop your manna and return to your side immediately.**
4) **Important! You must touch the team's box—on your side—before returning to play.**

QUICK TIP!

Joseph keeps running with his manna even though he's been tagged. Say, "Joseph, when you're tagged, drop your manna right away. That's part of the game! Then, quick, return to your side. Can you show me how it's done?" Children may need to sit out and watch a round of play, if they continue to disregard game rules.

FIELD TEST TIP!

This running game works best on grass or carpeted floor to cushion falls.

FIELD TEST TIP!

Position the chairs near the borders of your game space for a longer play area.

Cosmic Clue Quest

Today's Cosmic Clue Quest takes place at Asteroid Alley. As kids arrive, encourage them to find the day's clues by looking for the stars that you've hidden throughout your space. (Younger children may need your help searching.) Once all the clues are located, have children read each one aloud and work as a group to unscramble the phrase. Then ask Space Voyagers to open their *Student Books* to page 10 and write the day's clues on the appropriate lines. (Younger children may again need help reading and writing the clues. Be sure that your teen helpers make themselves available to assist as needed.) After every child has recorded the day's clue, ask a few kids to re-hide the clues where they were found and remind the group not to share today's clue with friends outside this room.

Here's today's Cosmic Clue:
<u>O</u>   <u>Lord</u>

For more details on the Cosmic Clue Quest, refer to page 6 in this guide.

Players "are safe" once they get back to their side (with a piece of manna) without getting tagged.

To start the game call out, "Manna Madness." Have a Tour Host watch to make sure the children are following the rules to the game. Watch for the team who collects all of their manna first. Have the entire group give the winning team a round of applause and some enthusiastic cheering before starting the game again. To play the game again, spill the manna from the boxes and spread it across the playing area.

Re-entry: Questions That Bring It Home

★ What was the most challenging part of this game? Did you feel like complaining during the game? Why?

★ Why did the Israelites complain while they were in the desert? How would you have acted if you were in the desert with them?

★ Think of three ways that God has provided for your needs today.

QUICK TIP!
Sometimes it's hard to tell who is on which team. Use streamers tied to upper arms to help determine the different players.

FIELD TEST TIP
If a "standoff" occurs or the game is taking too long, try designating five seconds as a "no-tag" time.

QUICK TIP!
Once you've explained the game, ask a few volunteers to demonstrate. Walk the volunteers through a brief demonstration, reviewing the game's rules as you go.

SUPPLIES

* Small craft feathers, one per child
* Cotton balls
* Sandwich bags, one per child
* Timer
* Bible

PREP TIME

5 minutes

Game Option 2: Birds and Bread Blastoff

GOAL

Keep feathers on heads, shoulders, knees, or noses while collecting "manna."

DO AHEAD

Spread cotton balls throughout the playing area.

QUICK TIP!

If playing this game outdoors, weight each feather using tape and a penny or substitute large craft sticks.

FIELD TEST TIP

Older Space Voyagers will be able to handle balancing the feathers on even trickier body parts, such as the bridge of their noses.

FIELD TEST TIP

Keep an eye out for players who may try and stick their feathers in ball caps and head-bands!

Ready, Set, Blast Off!

In our Bible story today we're learning that birds called quail and bread called manna were two things God provided for the Israelites. The Israelites were God's people living in the desert. They were hot, thirsty, and hungry. They cried out to God to help them with their needs. God heard their cries. In the mornings God provided manna, which was like bread. The manna would show up with the morning dew. The people would go out in the morning and gather the manna. They would collect just enough manna for the day. God also provided meat for the people to eat. How did God do this? At night God would send quail. Quails are a type of bird. The people would cook the birds, which would provide them with meat to eat. The people had a need; they were hungry. God provided for the people. He supplied them with what they needed. He provided manna and quail for the people to eat.

Let's play a game that will remind us of the manna and quail that God sent to provide for the needs of the Israelites. The Israelites counted on God, and we can count on God too. Have the children repeat the **Live It!** statement with you: **God is awesome! I can count on him.**

Point to the cotton balls on the playing area. **Cotton balls will remind us of the manna God sent in the mornings for the Israelites to collect.** Hand out a sandwich bag to each child. **These small bags will hold the manna you'll collect during the game.** Hand a feather to each child. **How do feathers remind us of today's Bible story?** Again, pause for answers. **Yes! The quail God sent at night so that the Israelites would have meat to eat.**

Let's play. Collect all the manna you can while balancing your feather on your _____. (Choose a body part such as elbow, knee, head, or shoulder. Be sure to demonstrate.) **If your feather falls to the ground, you must empty your manna bag and start over. After a few minutes we'll see who has gathered the most manna.**

Demonstrate how to keep the feathers on your elbow, knee, head, or shoulders. For a different challenge, have older children try to keep a lightweight down feather in the air by blowing on it—all while trying to scoop up lots of manna.

QUICK TIP!

Playing praise music, such as songs from the *Cosmic City*™ *Praise Songs* CD, helps create a fun atmosphere as kids collect the manna. Stopping the music can also indicate the end of play. (Order copies of the *Cosmic City*™ *Praise Songs* CD at www.cookvbs.com.)

Remind everyone which body part the feather must go on before play starts. To begin, have the whole group join you in counting down from 10 to 0. Time the group for two minutes, then have the children sit, empty their bags, and count their cotton balls. The person with the most cotton balls wins. Play as many times as you wish. To begin play again, collect the cotton balls and spread them out on the playing area. Make sure every child has a baggie and a feather. You may also want to specify a different body part each time a new game starts.

Re-entry: Questions That Bring It Home

* What was the most challenging part of this game? Did you ever complain or feel like complaining during the game? Why?
* Why did the Israelites complain while they were in the desert? How would you have acted if you were in the desert with them?
* Think of three different ways that God has provided for your needs today.

Healing Wonder

BIBLE STORY
Jesus Heals a Paralyzed Man (Luke 5:17–26)

KEY VERSE
You are the God who performs miracles; you display your power among the peoples. (Ps. 77:14)

LIVE IT! **God is awesome! I can believe in him.**

SUPPLIES
* 4 small carpet squares (2' x 3') or welcome mats or bath towels
* 4 chairs
* 4 clean long socks (or long strips of paper towels or streamers)
* Masking tape/cones
* Bible

PREP TIME
5 minutes

Particles from the sun fly toward Earth at close to a million miles per hour … what power![3]

Game Option 1: Mat Mix–up

GOAL
Get safely back "home" with your mat.

DO AHEAD
Use masking tape or safety cones to create a square playing area, approximately 15 x 15 feet. Place a carpet square or towel in each corner, and a chair in the center of each side of the playing square.

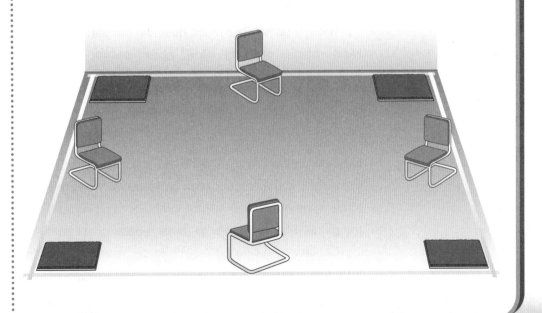

[3]Mark R. Chartrand, *Planets* (New York: Golden Guides for St. Martin's Press, 1990), 37.

Ready, Set, Blast Off!

Our Bible story is about Jesus and an amazing miracle. Jesus was teaching in a small village. Men had heard Jesus was in town. They were excited because Jesus was known for performing miracles. The men had a friend who could not walk because he was paralyzed. The men thought, "If we can just get our friend to see Jesus, Jesus will heal him."

So the men put their friend on a mat so they could carry him to see Jesus. But when they got to the house where Jesus was, there were so many people they couldn't get to Jesus. The men were worried that Jesus might not see their friend. So they came up with a plan. They went up on the roof of the house. They cut a hole in the roof, and then they lowered their friend on his mat through the roof—right in front of the spot where Jesus was standing.

When Jesus saw what the men did to help their friend, he was amazed and said to the paralyzed man, "Friend, your sins are forgiven." Jesus forgave the man of all the wrongs he'd ever done—wow! But Jesus didn't stop there; he went on to heal the man's body just as the friends knew he would. Jesus told the man to pick up his mat and go home.

Can you imagine if you were this man? All of a sudden you're forgiven of every sin you'd ever committed. Then in the next moment, your body is healed, and Jesus tells you to pick up your mat and go home. The man was so excited he immediately picked up his mat and went home, praising, thanking, and worshipping God the whole way. God is so awesome! He is so powerful he can heal people.

Have the children repeat the **Live It!** statement with you: **God is awesome! I can believe in him.**

Today's game uses mats. Just like the paralyzed man picked up his mat and went home praising God after Jesus healed him, we're going to pick up mats and head for home too.

Select four children to be "runners." Have each child tuck the end of a sock into the back pocket or waistband of his or her clothing. Make sure a good amount of the sock is sticking out, like a tail. Then have each player sit in a chair. **Your chair is home base.** Ask players to point to the mat in the corner that's farthest from him or her and to the right. **Your goal is to pick up your mat, head to that far corner and get back home—without having anyone grab your tail! If your tail is grabbed you're out of the game. The first player to make it back home safely is the winner.**

Choose three different players to be "roamers." **The "roamers" will pull socks from the "runners." Let's play.** Shout, "Mat Mix-up!" to start play.

Launch Farther!

If you have a large group of children, break into four teams. Place each team in one of the corners of the playing area. Select the players from the teams to be the participants. You may wish to have a Tour Host keep track of which team wins the most, enabling you to announce an overall winner.

Once children understand the game, set a two-minute play time. Rotate children in and out of the game so everyone gets a chance to play. Those not playing during a particular round should stay outside of the playing area and cheer. Remind children to keep their cheers positive. For more challenging play, move the mats farther away or add more taggers or runners to the mix.

Re-entry: Questions That Bring It Home

✳ If you were the paralyzed man whom Jesus healed, what's the first thing you would've done after picking up your mat and walking home?

✳ Why do you think Jesus forgave the paralyzed man before healing his body?

✳ In today's Bible story, the paralyzed man's friends brought him to Jesus to be healed. They worked as a team because they cared about their friend. How would today's game have been different if you were allowed to work as a team and help each other out?

FIELD TEST TIP
Be sure your "runners" have a waistband to hold the game socks. Girls in dresses, for example, make better "roamers" than "runners."

QUICK TIP!
If your group is larger than 20, set up two playing areas.

FIELD TEST TIP
For play on grass, use spray paint to mark off the playing boundaries.

SUPPLIES

* 30-gallon yard and leaf trash bags, one per team
* Masking tape
* Scissors
* Bible

PREP TIME

5 minutes

Game Option 2: Mega Mats

GOAL

Work together to make it "home" with your mat.

DO AHEAD

Cut open the sides of each bag to make two long mats. Use tape to mark the start and finish lines, approximately 15 feet apart.

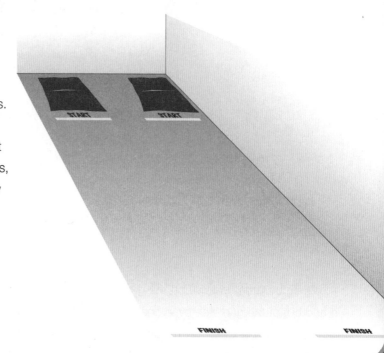

Ready, Set, Blast Off!

Imagine what it would be like if you couldn't walk. In our Bible story today we learned about a man who couldn't walk; he was paralyzed. Today people who are paralyzed can often move around in wheelchairs. But during Bible times, people didn't have wheelchairs. This man could only move around if his friends helped carry him on a mat. This man had some terrific friends who wanted to help him.

His friends believed Jesus was the Son of God and had the power to heal people. So when his friends heard Jesus was in town, they took him to see Jesus. When they arrived at the house where Jesus was, there were many people already there. There were so many people the man's friends couldn't get close to Jesus.

Remember when I said this man had terrific friends? Well, his friends were determined to see Jesus. So they went up on the roof of the house where Jesus was. Then they cut a hole in the roof of the house. They placed their friend on a mat and lowered him down through the hole. He landed right in front of Jesus.

QUICK TIP!

You can play this game with two or more teams at once.

QUICK TIP!

If desired, you can substitute large beach towels for the trash bags.

When Jesus saw the man, he said to him, "Friend, your sins are forgiven." But Jesus didn't stop at forgiving him for every wrong he had ever committed; he went on to heal the man's body. Jesus was the Son of God and had the power to heal the man, both on the inside and outside.

After Jesus healed him, Jesus told the man to pick up his mat and to go home! Can you imagine? Not being able to walk and then suddenly having Jesus tell you to stand up, pick up your mat and go home! Well, the man did just that. He picked up his mat and went home. As he walked home he praised God and worshipped him. Have the children say the **Live It!** statement with you: **God is awesome! I can believe in him.**

Arrange the children in teams of two to four players. **Let's play a game with our friends. Each team will use a mega mat and a little teamwork to try and go home just like the man in the Bible story picked up his mat and went home.**

Each team will start by standing on their mega mat at their start line. Point to the start lines. **Everyone must be on the mat at all times and cannot step off. As a team, figure out a way to move your mat without stepping off it.**

Launch Farther!

This game will be very challenging, so encourage the children to work together. As the teams problem solve, add more challenging aspects. For example, tell them that all of the team members must stand on the mat using only one leg.

FIELD TEST TIP

Have older kids read portions of today's Healing Wonder story (Luke 5:17–26) from your Bible before and after play to reinforce the awesome power of God's Word.

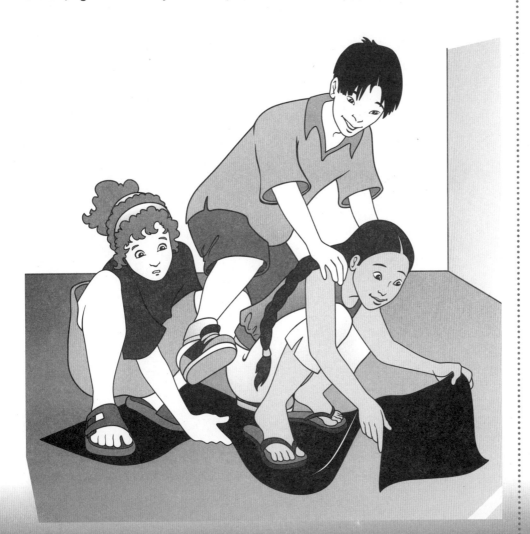

Point to the finish lines, or "home." **The first team to reach home on their mega mat wins the game.** Give a signal to start the challenge. Have a Tour Host or teen helper watch to make sure that everyone stays on their mats.

Re-entry: Questions That Bring It Home

* If you were the paralyzed man whom Jesus healed, what's the first thing you would've done after picking up your mat and walking home?
* Why do you think Jesus forgave the paralyzed man before healing his body?
* In today's Bible story, the paralyzed man's friends brought him to Jesus to be healed. They worked as a team because they cared about their friend. How did you work as a team in today's game? What was challenging about working as a team?

Water Wonder

BIBLE STORY
Jesus Walks on Water (Matt. 14:22–33)

KEY VERSE
All things are possible with God. (Mark 10:27)

LIVE IT! God is awesome! I can trust in him.

SUPPLIES
* Masking tape
* Plastic play hoops, one per team
* Small tarp (approx. 8' x 10')
* 40 balloons
* Spray water bottles
* Bible

PREP TIME
10 minutes

Out of this World!
The Hubble telescope has helped scientists see things in space that we thought would be impossible to see. The telescope is nearly the size of a large school bus, but it can fit inside a space shuttle's cargo bay.[4]

Game Option 1: Row, Row, Row your Boat

GOAL
Cross the "water" and gather balloons.

DO AHEAD
Blow up the balloons. Use tape to mark off a large square playing area. The bigger the square, the more challenging the game. Place the tarp in the center of the square and the balloons on the tarp. Place the hoops as shown.

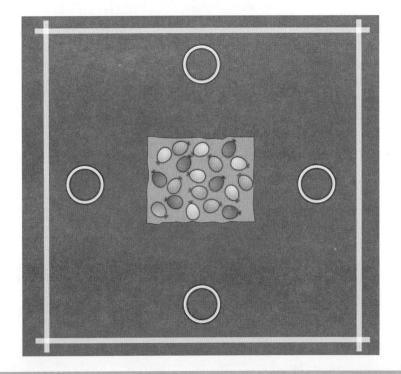

Ready, Set, Blast Off!

Have you ever been surprised? I mean *really* surprised by something you didn't expect at all? Like when someone jumps out and scares you? Why does it scare you? Probably because it was something you didn't expect.

Well, today's Bible story is about the disciples and a surprise that gave them a really good scare. Jesus had been teaching all day long. He and his disciples were pretty tired. So Jesus told the disciples to get into their boat, and he would join them in a little while. Jesus went off to pray while the disciples floated in their boat. After some time had passed the boat was a little too far off the shore. So Jesus decided to walk out to the boat. Wait a minute … did I say walk out on the *water*? That's what I said, and that's exactly what Jesus did. He walked on the water, right out to the disciples who were sitting in their boat.

Do you think they were surprised? Pause for kids to answer. **Do you think they were expecting Jesus to walk right up to their boat?** Again, pause and wait for kids to shout out, "No!" **Show me how you think their faces might have looked as they saw Jesus walking toward them.** Give time for children to make faces. You may even

ALLERGY ALERT

Balloons may pose a problem for children with latex allergies. Check with kids before play.

Launch Farther!

You if choose, substitute rope circles for the plastic hoops. Tie the ends of the ropes together to form circles about the same diameter as the hoops. You might wish to have a backup rope "hoop" ready in case a plastic hoop breaks. Plastic hoops are definitely more challenging—and fun!

Launch Farther!

To add more excitement to the game, equip each team with a spray water bottle. Set the following rule: Once squirted, the team must return their balloon to the center of the playing area.

want to demonstrate a terrified look of your own. **Jesus saw their faces too! He knew they were afraid. Jesus told them not to be afraid, but to trust him. After seeing this, the disciples were truly amazed. They worshipped and trusted God.** Have the children repeat the **Live It!** statement with you: **God is awesome! I can trust in him.**

Let's play a game where you need to stay in your boat. This game will remind us of the miracle that occurred when Jesus walked on the water. Jesus could walk on the water because he is the Son of God. Have the children get into teams of four to six players. Each team should be placed on each of the four sides of the square. You can play this game with as few as two teams, each on opposite sides of the square.

Give each team a hoop. Have all the members of the team stand in the plastic hoop with the hoop at about waist high.

The hoop is your boat. Once you cross your sideline you've entered the water—otherwise known as the splash zone. You can have one or two Tour Host or Guides spray the groups with water when they're in the splash zone. There's no penalty for getting splashed.

Together you must travel to the center of the square and pick up one balloon. Pick up only one balloon at a time. Once you have a balloon, return to your side and drop the balloon. Then go back into the water and retrieve another balloon. Continue to row, row, row your boats until all the balloons are gone. The team with the most balloons on their side at the end of the game wins. Begin the game by shouting out, "**Row, row, row your boats!**"

The larger the group, or older the kids, the more challenging it will be to have everyone work together inside the play hoop. To start the game over, collect the balloons and return them to the center of the square. Have groups start on their designated side of the square and begin play again.

Re-entry: Questions That Bring It Home

✸ If you had been in the boat with the disciples, what would you have done when you saw Jesus walking on water?

✸ Has God ever helped you do something that seemed impossible? Tell a partner about this time.

✸ What was the most challenging part of today's game? What do you think was the most challenging (or perhaps the scariest) thing for Peter about stepping out of the boat?

SUPPLIES

✱ Masking tape
✱ 2 buckets of water
✱ 10 small sponges
✱ 20 large paper grocery bags
✱ Bible

PREP TIME

10 minutes

Game Option 2: Walk on Water Dash

GOAL

Dash across the water without getting wet.

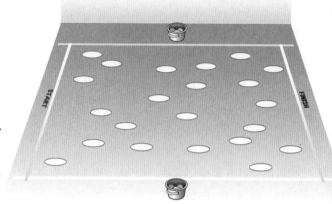

DO AHEAD

Use the tape to mark off a rectangular playing area (20' x 15'). Indicate the start and finish lines on the short ends of the playing area. Place sponges in buckets and leave them just outside the playing area, along the middle of the long sidelines. Cut the bags into large ovals (you'll get two ovals for each bag) for a total of forty large ovals. Spread the paper ovals throughout the playing field.

Ready, Set, Blast Off!

FIELD TEST TIP

Before playing, demonstrate a "good" tag for each game group. The sponge should be thrown softly and below the shoulders. Tell kids you're looking for players who are "good" taggers.

Peter was on a boat with the other disciples in the middle of a lake during a horrible storm. The wind was howling and the waves were crashing violently. But in the midst of the storm, Jesus took off across the lake to join them. Amazingly, Jesus walked on water!

The disciples were terrified because they'd never seen anything like it. When Peter realized that the man coming towards them was Jesus, he stepped out and started walking toward him.

But then Peter took his eyes off Jesus. He noticed the giant waves and water all around him and realized how dangerous the situation seemed. So Peter started to sink like a rock. Just then, Jesus reached out and grabbed Peter's hand, and Peter stopped sinking. Next, Jesus helped Peter climb back into the boat. The disciples were amazed by what they just saw. Jesus truly is the Son of God. He truly is worthy of our trust. Have the children say the **Live It!** statement with you: **God is awesome! I can trust in him.**

Have all the children sit on the start line. **In this game, you'll dash across the water trying not to sink like a rock! Between this shore** (point to where you're standing) **to the other shore** (point across the playing area) **is water. The object of** the game is to get to the opposite side safely—without being tagged by a wet sponge. Go to a bucket and pick up a sponge. **Players will tag you by touching you with the sponge or by tossing the sponge at you. If you're tagged while in the water, go back to the start line.**

Point to the paper ovals. **Now these paper ovals are rocks. As long as you're standing on a rock, you're safe. If you get tagged by a sponge while you're standing on a rock, you don't have to go back to start. You can continue to dash to the other side. Ready for play?**

Select a Tour Host to be the first player to tag. On your command, start the game. The player who's tagging can run anywhere on the playing field. Once everyone makes it to the other side, start the game again. The first player to the other side wins.

Make the winner of the game the tagger for the next game. To make the game more challenging, add two or three more taggers per game. Or don't allow the taggers to enter the playing field unless they pick up a sponge. In this case, to tag someone taggers must throw the sponge from outside the lines of the playing field.

Launch Farther!

Substitute foam balls or small kick balls for balloons and sponges for inside play. This will make the task of tagging people a little more challenging as balls will roll outside of the playing area. You might want to have two or more people to do the tagging.

Re-entry: Questions That Bring It Home

✱ If you had been in the boat with the disciples, what would you have done when you saw Jesus walking on water?

✱ Has God ever helped you do something that seemed impossible? Tell a partner about this time.

✱ What was the most challenging part of today's game? What do you think was the most challenging (or perhaps the scariest) thing for Peter about stepping out of the boat?

DAY 5

The Wonder of God Brought Down to Earth

BIBLE STORY
Jesus' Resurrection (John 19:1–6, 16–18; 20:1–18)

KEY VERSE
I want to know Christ and the power of his resurrection. (Phil. 3:10)

LIVE IT! God is awesome! I can tell others about Jesus.

SUPPLIES
* 10–14 balloons per team
* Small tarp (approx. 8' x 10')
* Masking tape, one roll per team
* Rolls of streamers, one per team
* Bible
* Optional: large trash bags

PREP TIME
10 minutes

QUICK TIP!
When blowing up balloons, you can place them into large trash bags for storage. This way you can have balloons ready if you choose to play the game more than once.

Out of this World!
The ISS, or International Space Station, is in orbit around the Earth. Modules that fit together to form the area where the astronauts live are being added to it until the year 2010.[5]

Game Option 1: Pass It On

GOAL
Form a cross using tape, streamers, and balloons.

DO AHEAD
Blow up the balloons. Place the tarp in the center of the playing area, and put all of the balloons on the tarp. From each side of the tarp mark off 10–15 feet and place a tape line about a foot long. These lines will serve as each teams' start lines. The teams will be facing the tarp. Behind each of the teams' start line, place a roll of tape and a roll of streamers.

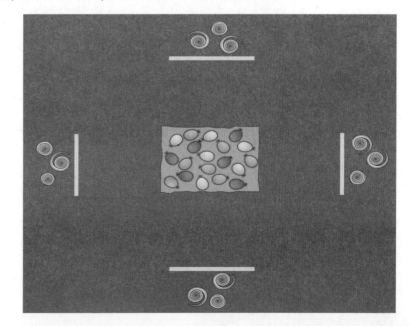

ALLERGY ALERT

Balloons may pose a problem for children with latex allergies. Check with kids before play.

QUICK TIP!

Use an air pump (such as those used for inflating basketballs or air mattresses) to blow up balloons or invite volunteers (teens work great) to help inflate balloons before the day's VBS starts.

FIELD TEST TIP

Have older kids read portions of today's Resurrection story (John 19:1–6, 16–18; 20:1–18) from your Bible before and after play to reinforce the awesome power of God's Word.

Ready, Set, Blast Off!

Good news! Good news! Very good news! What do you do when you hear good news? Do you run out and tell others? Or do you pick up the phone and tell someone about it? I know I do.

In our Bible story today, Mary and the disciples learned great news. Their news is so good we still want to pass it on today. What is their good news? Well, at first the news wasn't so good. Mary and the disciples had been friends with Jesus, and Jesus was just put to death on a cross. This was some very sad news.

After Jesus was buried in a tomb, Mary and the disciples went to visit the tomb. But when they got there, the tomb was empty. Why was the tomb empty? The tomb was empty because Jesus was no longer dead. He was alive. This was incredible news! Mary and the disciples were so happy, they had to tell everyone the good news that Jesus was alive. We can pass on the good news too. Have the children say the **Live It!** statement with you: **God is awesome! I can tell others about Jesus.**

Divide the children into teams. You can have two to four teams playing at the same time. Your teams can also be as small as three people or as large as the playing area will allow. Have each team sit one person behind the other at their start line, facing the tarp and balloons.

Let's play a game where you pass on the good news to your teammates just as Mary and the disciples passed on the *really* good news of Jesus' resurrection to others. When I say, "Pass it on," your team will form a line, one person behind the other, between the tarp and your team's line. The first person in line will pick up a balloon and pass the balloon between his or her legs to the next person.

The person reaching for the balloons cannot step on the tarp to reach a balloon. Only one balloon may be picked up at time. Once that balloon is passed, the first person can pick up another. That person will then pass it on between his or her legs to the next person, until the balloon has passed between everyone's legs. The last person will pass the balloon between his or her legs and drop the balloon behind the line.

Depending on the number of players, teams will have to move, scooting up or back to get to each player and to have the last player drop the balloon behind the line. **If a balloon touches the floor while it's being passed, you must return that balloon to the tarp by passing the balloon overhead. Keep passing balloons until the tarp is empty. When the last balloon being passed on your team crosses the line, the whole team then comes together.**

Your challenge is not over yet! Your team must then use the tape, the streamers, and the balloons to build a cross. Each team will be judged according to three categories: the best cooperation, the biggest cross, and the most creative cross. Your team's goal is to be the lead in at least one of these categories. Summarize the main points of the game. **Let's review the game.**

1. **Teams pass the balloons between their legs to the person behind them.**
2. **The first player in line cannot step on the tarp to reach the balloons.**
3. **The balloons cannot touch the ground. If they do, they have to be passed overhead back to the tarp.**
4. **Once the tarp is empty and your last balloon has crossed the line, the whole team goes behind the line. Finally, build a cross using the tape, streamers, and balloons.**

Launch Farther!

As the balloons are passed, have the players shout, "Jesus lives!" or "Good news, Jesus lives!"

Launch Farther!

For outside play, use boxes to hold the balloons, especially if it's a windy day. You'll need a large box instead of the tarp and smaller boxes behind each team.

QUICK TIP!

Enlist your teen helpers as judges, and encourage them to have fun with the judging process. Keep it lighthearted!

Re-entry: Questions That Bring It Home

- **Imagine that you were the first person to visit Jesus' empty tomb. Who would you tell the good news to first? What would you say?**
- **Jesus died and then rose again! What amazes you most about this news?**
- **Your team built a cross during today's game. When you see a cross, what do you think of? Why?**

SUPPLIES

✶ 22 large foam cups per team
✶ 2 beach towels per team
✶ Bible

PREP TIME

5 minutes

Game Option 2: Criss-cross

GOAL

Work as a team to build a cross.

DO AHEAD

Each team will start with a cross made of cups set up on one towel. Place the cups upside down in the pattern indicated. Place the other towel in a different location, preferably where the teams will have to cross each others' paths. The closer the towels are to everyone else's, the crazier and more challenging the criss-cross activity will be.

Ready, Set, Blast Off!

In our Bible story today we learned that Jesus came down to Earth for one reason—to save people. He did this through his death and his resurrection. Jesus died on a cross to pay the penalty for our sins and give all people the chance to live forever in heaven. Better yet, three days after Jesus died, he came back to life. Jesus rose from the grave because he was God's Son. We know that Jesus is alive because Mary Magdalene and Simon Peter and others saw the proof. He wasn't in the grave. He had risen just as he said he would.

This was great news that Mary and the others could not keep to themselves. So they began to tell others of the great news. Jesus is the Son of God. Jesus is alive and can save you from your sins. Have the children say the **Live It!** statement with you: **God is awesome! I can tell others about Jesus.**

Divide the children into small groups of two to four players. Have each group sit next to a towel with a cross of cups already set up.

Let's play a game where you work together to build a cross. See the cross? What does it remind you of? Give children a chance to share their thoughts. It reminds me of Jesus. It reminds me of what Jesus did for us. Jesus died for our sins on the cross, but now he lives. You'll help each other by picking up this cross one cup at a time and moving it across the room to your other team towel. Point out to each team the other towel across the room.

On your other towel build your cross again. You can only carry one cup at a time. Your cross must look just like the cross you started with. When I say, "Criss-cross," begin. The team who finishes building their cross first wins.

Re-entry: Questions That Bring It Home

✳ Imagine that you were the first person to visit Jesus' empty tomb. Who would you tell the good news to first? What would you say?

✳ Jesus died and then rose again! What amazes you most about this news?

✳ Your team built a cross during today's game. When you see a cross, what do you think of? Why?

QUICK TIP!

Foam cups work well for this indoor game. To play this game outside on a windy day, use foam cups weighted with bean bags or heavy plastic drinking cups or large wooden blocks.

Notes

Notes

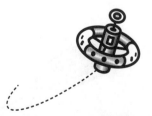

Notes